T0177069

# Who Is
# Ariana Grande?

# Who Is
# Ariana Grande?

by Kirsten Anderson

illustrated by Gregory Copeland

Penguin Workshop

To all the animal rescuers—thank you for
everything you do. (Adopt, don't shop.)—KA

PENGUIN WORKSHOP
An imprint of Penguin Random House LLC, New York

First published in the United States of America by Penguin Workshop,
an imprint of Penguin Random House LLC, New York, 2024

Visit us online at penguinrandomhouse.com.

Library of Congress Cataloging-in-Publication Data is available.

Printed in the United States of America

ISBN 9780593889015 (paperback)          10 9 8 7 6 5 4 3 2 1 CJKW
ISBN 9780593889022 (library binding)     10 9 8 7 6 5 4 3 2 1 CJKW

# Contents

# Who Is Ariana Grande?

It's always busy backstage at a Broadway musical, especially after the show. Actors rush to get out of their costumes and makeup. The stage crew works on getting all the sets and props ready for the next show.

To add to the backstage buzz, there might be visitors. Maybe they are friends or family of the cast and crew. Others might be famous actors, musicians, or politicians who want to see the new performance. Sometimes there are even lucky fans of the show excited to meet the many people who make the musical so great.

One night in 2003, Kristin Chenoweth, who starred as Glinda in the new hit show *Wicked*, was asked to meet a fan who had won a contest to come backstage. The small ten-year-old girl with

1

dark curly hair was there with her grandmother. When they met, the excited girl told Kristin, "I want to be you."

Chenoweth smiled. She had heard that from many young fans. But it takes a lot of hard work, patience, and talent to make it on Broadway.

Then, the girl's grandmother told her to sing. Without hesitation, the young fan broke out into "Popular," one of Glinda's songs. Kristin couldn't believe what she was hearing. The child's voice was strong and she hit every note easily. Impressed, the star gave the girl a wand from the show and took a picture with her.

That backstage visitor was named Ariana Grande.

In a few short years, she would be on Broadway herself. Soon after that, she would be a TV star. Then, she would launch one of the most successful pop music careers of her era. And around twenty years after that backstage visit, Ariana would get to live out the dream of a lifetime—starring in the movie version of *Wicked* as Glinda . . . the same role that she had seen Kristin Chenoweth perform years before.

Ariana Grande would have tragedies as well as triumphs along the way to completing the full circle from that moment backstage at *Wicked*. But before any of that happened, she was just a girl in Florida who loved to sing along with the radio in her mom's car.

# CHAPTER 1
## Broadway Bound

Ariana Grande-Butera was born on June 26, 1993, in Boca Raton, Florida. Her mother, Joan Grande, ran a communications technology company. Her father, Ed Butera, was a graphic designer. She has an older half brother, Frankie.

Ariana grew up loving horror movies and scary things, just like her mom. They dressed up in creepy costumes and makeup even when it wasn't Halloween. One of her early birthday parties had a *Jaws* theme, with the classic movie about a killer shark playing on a big screen at their home. Many of the young guests got scared and left. But it didn't bother Ariana—*Jaws* was her favorite movie!

Ariana also showed an early interest in music.

She enjoyed watching old movie musicals starring famous singers like Judy Garland and also listened to all the popular songs of the 1990s and early 2000s.

Her favorite singers were Mariah Carey and Whitney Houston, two artists known for their powerful voices.

When Ariana sang her favorites, though, she didn't sound like most kids her age. Sometimes, as she sang with the car radio, her mom had trouble telling which voice was Ariana's and which was the professional singer's!

Ariana already had her eye on a career as a performer. She watched shows on Nickelodeon, a cable network for kids, and wanted desperately to be a part of them. When she was four years old, she called the network's office and asked how to get on the shows. The person she spoke with told her she needed an agent.

Even without an agent, people were starting to notice Ariana. She played Annie in the musical *Annie* at a community theater when she was just eight years old, then also appeared in *The Wizard of Oz* and *Beauty and the Beast* at that same theater.

Ariana performs in *Annie*

Around that time, Ariana's parents separated. It hurt Ariana to see her parents break up, but she had support from her mom, Frankie, and her beloved grandpa and nonna (the Italian word for grandmother).

Joan began to take Ariana to karaoke nights at restaurants so she could get more chances to sing. At karaoke nights, she could get up in front of a crowd and sing along to the musical tracks of her favorite songs.

One night, Gloria Estefan, one of the most popular singers of the 1980s and 1990s, happened to be at the karaoke lounge on a cruise ship that Ariana and her mother were vacationing on. She heard Ariana singing and was shocked by the power and range of her voice. After Ariana finished, Estefan went up to her and Joan. Estefan told them that Ariana should try to become a professional singer because she had an amazing voice.

What made Ariana's voice special? It sounded pretty, but what really caught people's attention was her big range. That meant that she could easily sing very low notes and very high notes in a strong voice. Ariana could even sing in what people call the "whistle range." That describes notes so high most people can only whistle them! It is very rare that people can sing in the whistle range as well as Ariana does.

Ariana also had learned from listening to her favorite singers Whitney and Mariah how to use her power and vocal range to show emotion by adding extra notes to a word in a song or holding a note longer than expected. That made her sound like a much more experienced performer.

In 2008, Ariana got her big break. A new Broadway show called *13: The Musical* was looking for young actors. The show was about the lives of thirteen-year-olds, and the producers were planning to cast real teenagers for all the roles.

# The Voice

Singers frequently talk about singing in their "chest voice" or "head voice." But what do they mean?

People use their larynx, a tube in their throat, to make sounds. When they make lower-pitched sounds, they feel vibrations across the lower muscle of the larynx. That's how it got the name "chest voice." When they make higher sounds, they feel those vibrations in the top muscle of the larynx. That's the head voice.

The chest voice is good for making loud sounds, like yelling. The head voice is usually lighter and thinner, but performers like opera singers learn how to add power to even the highest notes in the head-voice range.

Mariah Carey is famous for her impressively wide vocal range. Soul singer Minnie Riperton, Broadway musical actress Julie Andrews, and rock star Freddie Mercury were also known for their powerful high notes.

Mariah Carey

Even the orchestra would be all teen musicians. Ariana and Aaron Simon Gross, one of her closest friends, were among the many young performers who auditioned—and they both were cast!

Ariana was only fifteen. But she had already made one of her big dreams come true.

## CHAPTER 2
## Fan Favorite

In *13*, Ariana played a cheerleader named Charlotte. The musical officially opened on Broadway on October 5, 2008. Ariana loved the energy she got from performing in front of an audience. She became friends with the other cast members, especially Liz Gillies, another talented singer. The two girls would continue to be friends for a very long time after meeting during this show.

*13: The Musical* closed on January 4, 2009. The show opened the door for other opportunities, though, and in the fall of 2009, Ariana and Liz were cast in a new Nickelodeon comedy called *Victorious*, starring Victoria Justice. The show was about teens at a performing arts high school.

Ariana played Cat Valentine, a funny girl who often did or said silly things.

Ariana had to make a big change for the character, though. The show's creators wanted Cat to have deep red hair. This meant that every other week during the show's production, Ariana had to bleach, then dye her naturally dark brown hair. The process was very harsh, and it began to damage Ariana's own hair.

*Victorious* premiered on March 27, 2010. The first episode got the second biggest audience for a live-action show in the history of Nickelodeon. It was a hit, and the network ordered a second season.

Although playing Cat won Ariana many fans, she had already decided that she really wanted to focus more on music than on acting. She was taking voice lessons in order to learn how to keep her voice healthy and strong, and she was writing and recording her own songs in her spare time.

Ariana was also making a name for herself on social media. While some stars hired professionals to run their social media accounts, Ariana was fully in charge of hers. She posted frequently on Twitter and communicated easily with the fans who began to follow her. They loved how she posted about ordinary moments in her life and how she took time to respond to them.

Ariana seemed like someone they might really be friends with, not a TV star. Her fans eventually called themselves "Arianators."

Ariana posted videos of herself singing on YouTube as well. She performed songs by Adele, Rihanna, and Bruno Mars. The videos were viewed millions of times, and she became one of YouTube's most watched musicians.

Fans weren't the only ones watching, though. Her videos caught the attention of executives at Republic Records, and in August 2011, Ariana signed her first record deal with them.

Ariana's first single for Republic, "Put Your Hearts Up," was released in December. Although it had some success, Ariana wasn't happy. It was a simple, bouncy teen pop song that didn't fit her style. She wanted to perform more complicated, emotional music, like the '90s R&B songs she listened to while growing up.

Filming for the third season of *Victorious*

wrapped in 2012 and Nickelodeon decided not to renew the show for another season. The last episode ran on February 2, 2013.

But this didn't mean Ariana could focus on music full-time yet. She had been cast in a new Nickelodeon comedy, *Sam & Cat*, which began filming in January 2013. In this show, her *Victorious* character, Cat, forms a babysitting service with Sam Puckett, a character played by Jennette McCurdy from *iCarly*, another popular Nickelodeon show.

At the same time, Ariana was finishing up her first full album. After talking to Republic Records executives, they agreed to let her focus on the R&B sounds she preferred. The new album included many of the songs Ariana had been working on over the last few years, with ideas from other experienced producers and songwriters. Some, like the singer-songwriter Victoria Monét, became close friends with Ariana.

A producer gave Ariana a song called "The Way," and she decided to record it as a duet with rapper Mac Miller. While working together on

the song, Mac taught Ariana how to use different audio engineering tools. She discovered that she loved being in the studio and creating songs.

Ariana and Mac Miller perform together

"The Way" was released on March 25, 2013, and it reached number nine on the *Billboard* Hot 100 singles chart. *Billboard* magazine's charts track the popularity of singles, or songs, and full albums. When Ariana's first album, *Yours Truly*, was released on August 30 of that same year, it immediately went to number one on *Billboard*'s charts. Ariana was only the fifteenth female artist in history to have her debut album open at number one.

*Sam & Cat* had also become a hit. Nickelodeon had originally planned to make twenty episodes for the first season, but the show did so well with audiences that the network added another twenty episodes.

Ariana had a hit album, a successful TV show, and was one of the most popular performers on Twitter, with almost as many followers as megastars like Britney Spears and Beyoncé. Life was good. But it was about to get more complicated.

# CHAPTER 3
## Manchester

During the summer of 2013, Ariana completed a short tour to promote *Yours Truly*, and also served as the opening act for a few Justin Bieber concerts. In the fall, she had to go back to filming *Sam & Cat*.

By now, Ariana was wearing a red wig on the show. The process of bleaching and dying her hair over and over during the last few years had wrecked it. Off-screen, she felt like she couldn't even show her real hair anymore. Instead, Ariana added brown extensions to her hair that she wore pulled into a long high ponytail. It became her signature style.

In January 2014, Ariana announced that she was already working on her second album.

She was still committed to *Sam & Cat*, but rumors were flying about problems with the show. Some people said that Ariana and her costar Jennette McCurdy weren't getting along. Others said that both Jennette and Ariana wanted to move on to other projects. In July, the network announced that the show had officially ended. Ariana could finally focus on music full-time.

It seemed like Ariana's voice was everywhere in the spring and summer of 2014. "Problem," a duet with rapper Iggy Azalea, was released in April as the first song from her upcoming album. It reached number two on the *Billboard* charts. The next single, "Break Free," was also a top five hit. Released in August 2014, *My Everything* became Ariana's second number one album.

In February 2015, when she was only twenty-two years old, Ariana set off on her first big international tour. She used the tour to promote pet adoption, one of her favorite causes. Ariana adored dogs and had her own collection of rescue pups at home. One of her dogs, Toulouse, even traveled with her. During tour stops, Ariana held pet adoption events at her concert venues, and she paid the fees for any pets adopted at those locations. All of those dogs were adopted!

Then, trouble struck. Video taken over the July Fourth weekend showed Ariana and a friend in a donut shop. In the video, Ariana is seen licking donuts she hadn't paid for and making unkind remarks about Americans.

People were outraged and Ariana now appeared really rude to anyone who had seen the video. A few days later, Ariana apologized for her behavior and harsh words. She said that she loved America and was proud to be an American.

On Twitter, Ariana also noted that she needed to clean up the way she spoke sometimes. The incident was a reminder that she was no longer just sharing her life with a group of adoring fans on social media, but with the whole world.

There were other troubles. Rumors spread that Ariana had walked out on photo shoots and been rude to interviewers. People began to call her a diva. They meant she was demanding and self-centered.

Ariana felt that she was just outspoken and had been doing what she believed was best for her career. She thought that people expected a young female pop star to be sweet and obedient, and that a young male star would not be criticized the way Ariana had been for doing the same things. Ariana came from a family of strong women and had been taught to stand up for herself. She was quick to shut down interviewers who asked questions that she felt were silly or insulting, and she refused to stay silent when she felt something was wrong.

The truth was that Ariana disliked doing all the promotion work for her music. She often told people that she would rather be in the recording studio than at big fancy events. She loved making music but didn't love all the other things that came with it. What others saw as glamour felt like work to her. She really only cared about her music and her fans.

These negative stories didn't seem to hurt Ariana's popularity, though. Ariana kept working on new music. She finished recording her new album in January of 2016 and released the first single, "Dangerous Woman," on March 10. That weekend, she both hosted and was the musical guest on *Saturday Night Live*. Ariana really impressed audiences in a sketch that featured her ability to do impressions of other famous singers like Shakira and Britney Spears.

*Dangerous Woman* was released on May 20, 2016, and debuted at number two on the *Billboard* charts. The songs "Dangerous Woman" and "Side to Side" became top ten hits.

In August, Ariana and Mac Miller began dating. Although they had known each other for years, they had just been friends. Ariana enjoyed being with Mac. But she also knew that he struggled with alcohol and drugs. She worried about him when they weren't together.

In February 2017, Ariana began another international tour. After finishing all of the North American shows, Ariana brought the tour to Europe.

On May 22, 2017, Ariana and her dancers were exiting the stage just after the show at the Manchester Arena in England. Suddenly, there were popping sounds. Security rushed Ariana and her team out of the arena and onto buses. Later, they found out that a terrorist had set off a bomb in the arena. Twenty-two people were killed and dozens more were injured.

Ariana was completely devastated. She immediately postponed the rest of the tour and returned to Florida with her mom. On Twitter, she wrote, "broken. from the bottom of my heart, i am so so sorry. i don't have words." Ariana spent days in bed, crying. The thought that people had lost their lives just because they had come to see her was almost too much to bear.

She realized she had to do something, though. On June 4, Ariana returned to Manchester for One Love Manchester, a show she organized to raise money for families affected by the bombing.

Many popular musicians joined her, including Miley Cyrus, Justin Bieber, Katy Perry, and Coldplay. The concert raised around thirteen million dollars for the Manchester victims.

Ariana ended the show with an emotional performance of the classic song "Over the Rainbow," from *The Wizard of Oz*. As she sang, she tried not to cry.

# CHAPTER 4
## Thank U

Ariana finished the rest of the tour, then returned home. Without the shows to keep her busy, she was overwhelmed by her feelings about what had happened. She was depressed and had anxiety attacks. An anxiety attack is when a person feels intense fear in response to stress.

Talking to a therapist helped, but so did making music. Ariana poured her feelings into new songs. Some of them were about overcoming difficulties and dealing with anxiety, while others were about feeling powerful and finding happiness. Ariana said she didn't want to dwell on sadness. She wanted the album to be hopeful.

In April 2018, Ariana released the first song from the album, "no tears left to cry." The song was about being positive and moving on from bad times. It also began what would become another one of Ariana's trademarks: She would present most titles of her songs in lowercase style, similar to how many of her followers use language on social media. The track reached number three on the *Billboard* charts.

Ariana also made some changes in her personal life. In May 2018, she broke up with Mac Miller. Soon after, Ariana started to date actor and comedian Pete Davidson. In June, they became engaged.

When the new album *Sweetener* was released on August 17, it debuted at number one on the *Billboard* charts. Critics applauded the album. Some called it her best work yet.

It should have been a happy time for Ariana. She was having an extremely successful year. Instead, tragedy struck again.

On September 7, 2018, Mac Miller died of a

drug overdose. Ariana was heartbroken. Although they had no longer been dating, she still cared about him. He had been a huge part of her life and a good friend.

Ariana struggled to escape her sadness. It almost seemed like the words of her song "no tears left to cry" had come back to haunt her. She had plenty more tears to cry.

Ariana's closest songwriter and producer friends gathered in New York, where Ariana was living. They pointed out that there was a recording studio nearby. The group suggested that Ariana get into the studio, where she had always been happy, and start work on a new project.

With her friends by her side, Ariana completed a new album in just a few weeks. Ariana felt it was her most personal work so far. The songs, meant for older listeners, were about grief, trauma, and relationships. Being with her friends and working helped Ariana. She said that the process turned everything around in her life.

In October, Ariana broke off her engagement with Pete Davidson. Then, on November 3, she surprised her fans by releasing "thank u, next" the first song from her upcoming album. It became Ariana's first number one song.

On December 6, 2018, Ariana was named *Billboard* Woman of the Year, an honor given to a woman in music who had made important contributions to the business and inspired others. At the ceremony, Ariana gave a tearful, emotional speech. She talked about how strange it was that 2018 had been the best year of her career, but also the worst year of her life.

In February 2019, the top three songs on the *Billboard* charts all belonged to Ariana: "7 rings," "break up with your girlfriend, i'm bored," and "thank u, next." She was the first solo artist to accomplish this feat, and the first artist since the Beatles in 1964!

Ariana accepts the *Billboard* Woman of the Year Award

Ariana released the album *thank u, next* on February 8, 2019. Two days later, she won her first Grammy Award when *Sweetener* was named Best Pop Vocal Album.

The Sweetener World Tour began in March 2019. Ariana worked with the group Headcount to help concertgoers register to vote at stops on the tour. Ariana believed that it was important that Americans voted in elections so their voices would be heard.

One show that year was extra special. Ariana returned to Manchester for the first time since 2017. She told the audience that she was "overwhelmed" and "so nervous" to be back. But she also said, "Manchester holds a very special place in my heart." It always would.

# CHAPTER 5
## For Good

In January 2020, Ariana met real estate agent Dalton Gomez while looking to buy a house in the Los Angeles area. They soon started dating. When the COVID-19 pandemic lockdown began in March, they moved in together.

By April, Ariana was working on new music for her next album. She also collaborated with other musicians. In May, Ariana and Justin Bieber recorded the song "Stuck with U" as a fundraiser to help first responders like EMTs (emergency medical technicians), health-care workers, and firefighters. It raised over $3.5 million. A few weeks later, a new duet by Ariana and pop megastar Lady Gaga titled "Rain on Me" became a number one hit.

On October 23, Ariana released the song "positions" and it immediately went to number one on the *Billboard* charts. The video showed what it would be like if Ariana was president of the United States!

Ariana's fifth number one album, *Positions*, was released on October 30. Also geared toward older listeners, it was a light R&B/pop album about love and having fun in relationships. It seemed to match where she was in her own life. Ariana and Dalton Gomez announced that they were engaged in December 2020.

For Ariana, 2021 was an incredibly busy year. In March, she and Lady Gaga won the Best Pop Duo/Group Performance award at the Grammys for "Rain On Me." Then, in May, she and Dalton were married.

In September, Ariana became a coach on the popular TV talent show *The Voice*. Just a few months later, in November, she introduced her own line of beauty products, r.e.m. beauty. All the products were vegan, not tested on animals, and packaged in recyclable materials.

Ariana had one more big announcement left in 2021. News had spread in Hollywood that a movie version of the musical *Wicked* was finally going to be made. Being in *Wicked* had been a longtime dream of Ariana's, so she auditioned to play Glinda the Good Witch. Many other actors also wanted the role, including Amanda Seyfried and Dove Cameron. After a series of auditions, it was announced on November 4, 2021, that Ariana had gotten the part. The award-winning actor and singer Cynthia Erivo would play Elphaba, the Wicked Witch of the West. Both women were incredibly excited to work together on the movie.

The film's director and producer decided to split the famous musical into two films. The first began filming in November 2022 in England.

It continued until July 2023, when film and TV actors went on strike to fight for better pay and working conditions.

Ariana used her unexpected free time due to the strike to start recording new music. By this

time she'd also separated from Dalton Gomez. In October, their divorce became final.

On January 12, 2024, Ariana released the song "yes, and?" It became her eighth number one song. Soon after, she announced that her next

album would be released in early March. The title of the album would be *eternal sunshine*, inspired by the title of one of Ariana's favorite movies, *Eternal Sunshine of the Spotless Mind.*

After the actors' strike ended in November, Ariana finished filming *Wicked: Part 1*. The film would be released in November of 2024, and the second half would debut exactly a year later in 2025.

Ariana Grande continues to be one of the most successful musical artists of her time. She holds many records for song and album sales, and is one of the most followed people on social media. Ariana has never been afraid to stand up for what she believes in. She has supported causes like LGBTQIA+ rights, women's rights, racial equality, and animal welfare, and has spoken up for the need for laws that reduce gun violence. Her songs have addressed important issues like anxiety and mental health. She inspires her fans not just with her strength as a singer but as a person.

Ariana was once asked what message she had for her fans. Her words were simple and hopeful: "Everything's gonna be alright."

# Timeline of Ariana Grande's Life

| | |
|---|---|
| 1993 | Born on June 26 in Boca Raton, Florida |
| 2008 | Makes Broadway debut in *13: The Musical* |
| 2009 | Cast as Cat Valentine in Nickelodeon show *Victorious* |
| 2011 | Signs record deal with Republic Records |
| 2013 | Stars in new Nickelodeon show *Sam & Cat* |
| | Releases first album, *Yours Truly* |
| 2014 | Releases second album, *My Everything* |
| 2016 | Releases third album, *Dangerous Woman* |
| 2017 | Survives Manchester Arena bombing |
| | Organizes and performs in One Love Manchester concert to support victims of Manchester bombing |
| 2018 | Releases fourth album, *Sweetener* |
| 2019 | Releases fifth album, *thank u, next* |
| | Wins first Grammy award |
| 2020 | Releases sixth album, *Positions* |
| 2021 | Wins Best Pop Duo/Group Performance Grammy Award for "Rain on Me," a duet with Lady Gaga |
| | Introduces r.e.m. line of beauty products |
| 2022 | Begins filming *Wicked* |
| 2024 | Releases seventh album, *eternal sunshine* |
| | *Wicked: Part 1* is released |

# Timeline of the World

**1993** — Bomb explodes in the World Trade Center garage, killing six people

**2000** — First crew goes to live in the International Space Station

**2009** — US Airways 1549 makes a safe emergency landing in the Hudson River

**2011** — Massive earthquake and tsunami strike Japan

**2013** — First hamburger grown in a lab is cooked and eaten

**2015** — Almost two hundred countries produce the Paris Climate Accord

**2017** — Francois Gabart sails around the world in a record 42 days, 16 hours, 40 minutes, and 35 seconds

**2019** — Scientists produce the first image of a black hole

**2020** — COVID-19 pandemic begins

**2022** — ChatGPT, an artificial intelligence chatbot that can converse and write in familiar language, is introduced

**2023** — Earth has its hottest year on record

# Bibliography

Boardman, Mickey, and Justin Moran. "In Conversation: Troye Sivan and Ariana Grande." *Paper*. August 23, 2018. https://www.papermag.com/troye-sivan-ariana-grande-conversation-2#rebelltitem25.

Connor, Katie. "Ariana Grande Is Here to Save Us." *Elle*. July 11, 2018. https://www.elle.com/culture/music/a22094769/ariana-grande-sweetener-album-manchester-cover-story/.

Dugdale, Paul, dir. *Ariana Grande: excuse me, i love you*. Den of Thieves, 2020.

Fellers, Stephen. "N. Broward Prep Student Already 'Victorious.'" *Sun-Sentinel*. June 17, 2010. https://web.archive.org/web/20160531111413/http://articles.sun-sentinel.com/2010-06-17/news/fl-mcf-nickelodeon-0617-20100617_1_audition-victorious-prep.

Flores, Alfredo, dir. *Ariana Grande: The Dangerous Woman Diaries*. Good Story Entertainment, 2018.

Goodman, Lizzy. "Ariana Grande on Fame, Freddy Krueger, and Her Freaky Past." *Billboard*. August 15, 2014. https://www.billboard.com/music/music-news/billboard-cover-ariana-grande-on-fame-freddy-krueger-and-her-freaky-past-6221482/.

Haskell, Rob. "Ariana Grande on Grief and Growing Up." *Vogue*. July 9, 2019. https://www.vogue.com/article/ariana-grande-cover-august-2019.

Lapuma, Joe. "Ariana Grande: 'Shadow of a Doubt.' " *Complex*.
November 5, 2013. https://www.complex.com/music/a/joe-
la-puma/ariana-grande-interview-shadow-of-a-doubt-2013-
cover-story.

Laracy, Noah. "Ariana Grande: A *Backstage* Exclusive." *Backstage*.
August 15, 2012. https://www.backstage.com/magazine/
article/ariana-grande-back-stage-exclusive-64080/.

Martins, Chris. "Ariana Grande on Defending Female Pop Stars and
Staying Away from Drama." *Billboard*. May 19, 2016. https://
www.billboard.com/music/music-news/ariana-grande-
billboard-cover-story-dangerous-woman-avoiding-drama-
feminism-7377472/.

Sang, Zach. "Ariana Grande Talks Sweetener, Pete Davidson & Nicki
Minaj." Zach Sang Show. August 17, 2018. YouTube video,
48:22. https://www.youtube.com/watch?v=PviZLT7HPys.

Sang, Zach. "Ariana Grande 'thank u, next' interview." Zach Sang
Show. February 9, 2019. YouTube video, 1:23:36. https://www.
youtube.com/watch?v=fpl8v3jiuNU&t=1908s.

Tanzer, Miles. "Ariana Grande." *Fader*. May 30, 2018. https://www.
thefader.com/2018/05/30/ariana-grande-cover-story.

# YOUR HEADQUARTERS FOR HISTORY

Activities, Mad Libs, and sidesplitting jokes!
Discover the Who HQ books beyond the biographies